GIRLS AGAINST GIRLS

First published in 2009 by
Zest Books, an imprint of Orange Avenue Publishing
35 Stillman Street, Suite 121, San Francisco, CA 94107
www.zestbooks.net

Created and produced by Zest Books, San Francisco, CA
© 2009 by Orange Avenue Publishing LLC
Photographs © 2009 by King Morgan, www.kingmorgan.com

Typeset in Adobe Jenson Pro, Arial Black, Quay Sans, and Minya

Teen Nonfiction / Social Issues / Girls and Women

Library of Congress Control Number: 2008931234
ISBN-13: 978-0-9790173-6-0
ISBN-10: 0-9790173-6-X

CREDITS
EDITORIAL DIRECTOR: Karen Macklin
CREATIVE DIRECTOR: Hallie Warshaw
ART DIRECTOR: Tanya Napier
WRITER: Bonnie Burton
ADDITIONAL RESEARCH: Erika Stalder
EDITOR: Karen Macklin
PHOTOGRAPHER: King Morgan
COVER DESIGN: Tanya Napier
DESIGN AND PRODUCTION: Cari McLaughlin
TEEN ADVISORY BOARD: Carolyn Hou, Lisa Macklin, Maxfield J. Peterson,
                      Joe Pinsker, Hannah Shr

Printed in China
First printing, 2009
10 9 8 7 6 5 4 3 2 1

*Every effort has been made to ensure that the information presented is accurate.
Readers are strongly advised to read product labels, follow manufacturers' in-
structions, and heed warnings. The publisher disclaims any liability for injuries,
losses, untoward results, or any other damages that may result from the use of the
information in this book.*

GIRLS AGAINST GIRLS

Why We Are Mean
to Each Other
and
How We Can Change

Foreword

In today's culture, girls are told they aren't good enough the way they are. It feels like they can't escape the pressure to compete with each other, or with themselves. This dynamic is everywhere, from the hallways of high school to reality TV shows, as girls try to one-up each other no matter whether it's a Sweet 16 party or a boyfriend. It's become normal for girls to think that other girls are naturally their enemies — or soon will be.

While most people might laugh this off and say "girls will be girls," I don't think it's that funny. Girls are not intrinsically mean. We act that way out of feelings of insecurity and fear, or because we see ourselves portrayed that way by the media and then try to replicate what we think is expected of us. But when we constantly tear each other down, we lose out on the connection, support, and friendship that we can offer one another.

Of course, it doesn't have to be that way. We can do better — and that's what Bonnie Burton's book, Girls Against Girls, is about. It illuminates the ways in which we antagonize each other and teaches us how to better understand ourselves so that we can make a change right now!

I know that this book will open your eyes to ways we can work together to build up our self-esteem and create a more positive world. I needed this book when I was a girl. I am so glad it's here for you now.

Jess Weiner

Jess Weiner, author and advice columnist
www.withjess.com

Note From the Author

When I was suffering through school, I distinctly remember the unspoken politics of being a girl. You could be making plans with your best friend one week and being given the silent treatment the next. Or some girl you don't even know might make you the victim of a terrible rumor for no reason at all. I went through all of this, like everyone else.

I remember lots of awful things that happened to me. Once, one of my best pals started a rumor that I was planning to steal another girl's boyfriend, and suddenly people I didn't even know were staring me down. It took what seemed like forever for the truth to dismantle that lie, and I never knew why she started it in the first place. I also remember times when I was on the flipside — like when I was angry with a friend for ditching me at the mall, so I commented to a known gossiper that she was caught shoplifting. In a heartbeat, I ruined her rep just as that previous friend had ruined mine.

That's why this book is so important. It's the kind of book I wish I had back then — a manual for figuring out why we do the cruel things we do to each other. It also explains that we all have the ability to choose whether we want to be destructive or supportive. Sure, girls and women can be mean and spiteful. But we can also be positive, compassionate, and downright cool! Shouldn't we choose to be the latter?

Writing this book — and interviewing the amazing artists and athletes who are quoted inside — cemented for me how awesome all of us girls really are. I hope that reading it will leave you feeling as inspired as I felt after writing it.

Bonnie Burton, author
www.grrl.com

1
WHY
We Hurt
Each Other
9

2
METHODS
of Our
Meanness
29

3
BEARING
the Brunt
of It
55

4
CALLING
in
Reinforcements
71

5
STOPPING
the
Cycle
89

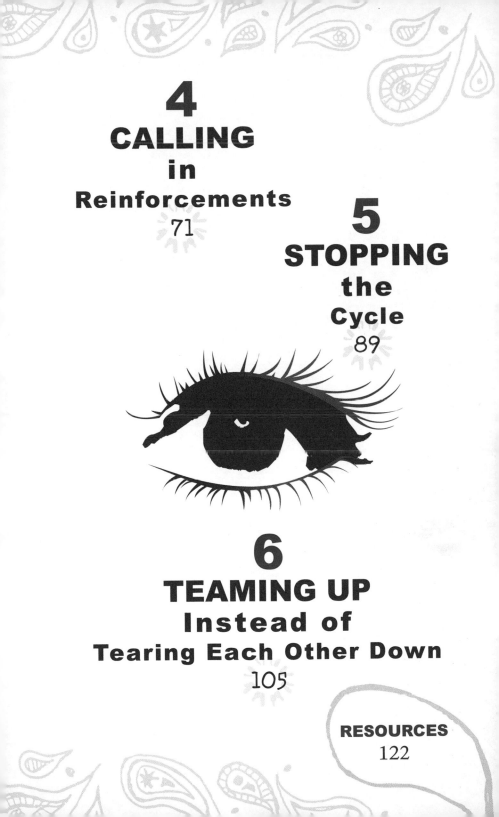

6
TEAMING UP
Instead of
Tearing Each Other Down
105

RESOURCES
122

1
WHY
We Hurt
Each Other

You've seen it in school, at camp, at home, and at your part-time job. We girls can be cruel. While most of us don't resort to slugging it out in the hallway or schoolyard, many of us do go for sneakier and more drawn-out types of infighting — like mind games, gossip, and rumor spreading. It happens so much that expressions like "Girls are mean" are favorites among our parents, brothers, and even ourselves.

Psychologists even have a name for the way we engage in emotional warfare: relational aggression. And unlike physical violence that's easy to spot, this type of girl drama can stay way below the radar. So parents and teachers often don't even see it happening and, if they do, don't take it seriously. Sometimes the girls who are psychologically beating up other girls don't even realize that they are, in fact, doing it.

You have probably been a victim—and a perpetrator. We all have. So the big question is: Why do we do it? Just like with anything, we have to understand the problem before we can find the solution. On the following pages are some theories about why we fight the way we do.

"You have no idea what someone else's life is like. The girl who looks like she has it all could have an eating disorder. Or someone could be getting abused at home. Understanding why people do what they do is crucial."

○ Kate Izquierdo ○

music editor, *San Francisco Bay Guardian*

<table>
<tr><td>theory</td></tr>
<tr><td>1</td></tr>
</table>

IT'S BIOLOGICAL

According to a number of scientists, some of our fighting is due to the way we are wired.

The Brain

Research has shown that the differences between women's and men's brains are very real, and that women's brains are much more complex than men's. Many scientists say that women, in general, are more communicative than men, have better facility with language, are more in tune with their emotions, have a stronger ability to sustain deep friendships, and have a better memory. These brain differences account for why women are so good at recognizing the emotions of others ("Honey, what's wrong?") and also for remembering every detail of an argument … forever ("You said I was fat, and you said it at precisely 8:15 pm on Friday night while you were wearing that ugly blue shirt with pinstripes").

Meanwhile, scientists say that boys cannot easily sense when someone is annoyed or upset with them or even remember what yesterday's fight was about, while girls are so in tune with everything going on around them that they observe and notice *everything*. This is a good quality in a lot of situations, but it also means that a girl will remember a hurtful comment for the next century, while a boy is more likely to forget about it by the next day.

Our Hormones

You have probably noticed that hormones affect
our brains big time, and during our teen years those
hormones, like estrogen and progesterone, start
seriously rising. The amount of hormones released
into our bodies (and brains) changes daily based on
our menstrual cycles, and researchers believe these
hormonal ebbs and flows affect our behavior, which
makes us want to bond with our friends during
certain parts of our cycle and kill them during others
(hello, PMS!).

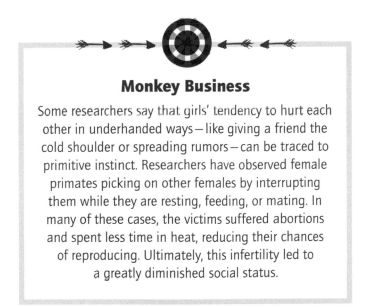

Monkey Business

Some researchers say that girls' tendency to hurt each
other in underhanded ways — like giving a friend the
cold shoulder or spreading rumors — can be traced to
primitive instinct. Researchers have observed female
primates picking on other females by interrupting
them while they are resting, feeding, or mating. In
many of these cases, the victims suffered abortions
and spent less time in heat, reducing their chances
of reproducing. Ultimately, this infertility led to
a greatly diminished social status.

Teen Brain

To top all of this off, there is the fact that you are a teenager, which simply means that your brain is in the middle of a crazy growth spurt.

Neuroscientists used to think human brains finished developing by age 6, but now they are saying that there is another brain growth spurt from age 11 to 20. During this time, the brain is firing 30,000 neural connections a minute in an effort to become more efficient. And where does much of this growth occur? In the prefrontal cortex — the area of the brain we use to make rational decisions. It's great for our minds to improve themselves, but that amount of work can turn our decision-making capabilities into mush. In fact, a teen's brain is more likely to get distracted and be ruled by emotion, leading to impulsive behavior. Then, poor judgments can be made, even by smart or normally confident people.

For instance, one day "Gina" walks into class and sees you and your friends huddled together and thinks she hears you say her name. Her rapidly growing prefrontal cortex might hastily tell her, "They're talking about you." Suddenly, she becomes self-conscious and irritated. Meanwhile, you were talking about geometry! From that day forward, you never understand why Gina won't speak to you.

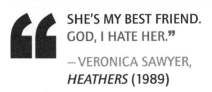

**SHE'S MY BEST FRIEND.
GOD, I HATE HER."**

—VERONICA SAWYER,
HEATHERS (1989)

The Good News

Even if these theories are true and we, as girls and
women, are somewhat "wired" to behave this way,
that doesn't mean we can't change. Many say that
men are wired for physical violence, dogs are wired
to bite people, and humans are wired for war. But if
we want to grow as a society, we have to realize that
we can change, grow, and refine aspects of ourselves
that don't serve us. After all, that's really what growth
and empowerment is all about: rising above it all.

WE ARE RAISED THIS WAY

When boys get angry or emotionally charged, they are often encouraged to let it out — either on the sports field or in the schoolyard. If your brother comes home with a black eye, it's almost expected: He's "just being a boy." But when girls get angry or emotionally charged, we are encouraged to rein it in.

Sugar and Spice

Society tells girls to always act properly, be sweet, and look pretty. We are encouraged to keep our ugly feelings inside — it doesn't look nice, after all, when a girl swats at other girls or swears and throws stuff around. In addition, parents often try to direct us away from aggression, not because they are trying to do us harm, but because they are trying to teach us to approach things rationally and peacefully. And, even when we know we've been wronged, we don't want to show anger for fear of losing friends. But let's face it: It's impossible to totally ignore feeling pissed off! So, instead of showing anger and other negative emotions, we bury them. Then those emotions sit there and marinate until the situation has spun entirely out of control.

Say your friend Ann did something small that hurt you, like invited another friend, Lori, to see your favorite band and didn't ask you. Instead of just letting Ann know that this upset you, you keep it inside for the sake of being "nice" and maintaining the friendship status quo. But you just can't help it — you still feel angry. So, to let it out, you tell someone else all the reasons you're upset with Ann. Then, that person tells someone else (with a few extra bits thrown in to make the story sound more interesting). Eventually, it travels along the school grapevine and finally reaches Ann, who had no idea she hurt you and isn't too thrilled that she's now viewed as a jerk by the rest of the school. Afraid to confront you (that wouldn't be "nice"), she just tells everyone that you're jealous of Lori. Before you know it, the situation is a huge mess.

Or remember the last time you were hurt by a friend's joke or comment but you didn't say anything ASAP? (After all, you wouldn't want her to think you were bitchy.) You lied to yourself that it wasn't a big deal — but it was, and you never stopped thinking about it. Then one day, she shows up five minutes late to meet you somewhere and you flip out. She thinks you're crazy for freaking out over five minutes, and you're all huffy because she doesn't have a clue that it's about the comment she made three months ago. See the problem?

This doesn't mean we should be slugging each other. It means we need to get better at communicating our feelings in a prompt and rational manner. Being falsely nice to friends simply to ward off potential conflict can create big problems later on.

"Passive-aggressiveness is particularly negative because it causes hurt without giving the person who is being hurt the opportunity to discuss the issue or defend themselves. It's also really cowardly. If you have a legitimate problem with someone, find the courage to address it in a way that keeps things out in the open."

Hannah Aitchison

tattoo artist and illustrator

theory
3

WE PASS DOWN THE LEGACY

One reason girls are cruel to each other is because older women have been cruel to them. Maybe a classmate's mom isn't even in her life, or her step-mom treats her like a second-class citizen, or her older sister tortures her at home. Unfortunately, she has decided to take it out … on you.

Or perhaps you are the one being treated harshly by an older woman? When a group of people has long been disempowered (like women), they may take out their frustrations on other, younger women as a way of exerting some power. If an older woman in your life is being mean to you, it may be for this reason. It may also be because she is threatened by you in some way or jealous because you have more opportunities than she did growing up. It could even be because she thinks that getting treated poorly by an older woman is a rite of passage for young girls. It can be hurtful to receive this kind of treatment — either from an older woman or from a peer who is taking her frustrations with abuse out on you — but if you can understand where the feelings are coming from, you may even be able to have some compassion for the person who is treating you so badly.

"All girls who
are mean to you are
scared and dealing with
something pretty terrible on the
inside that forced them to be so
cruel. One of the greatest 'Aha!'
moments I had was after I did the
The Oprah Winfrey Show in 2004 for my
first book. A lot of people I went to school with
came out of the woodwork to congratulate me. I
wrote very candidly in my book about the emotional
torture I endured by a certain group of girls at school.

"Well, the ringleader (who threw eggs at my house
during all of my birthday parties) wrote me an email to
apologize for being so mean to me, after she had seen me
on Oprah and had read my book. She said what I didn't
know at the time was that her mother's boyfriend had
been molesting her and she was so angry and full
of jealousy that I had two parents who were still
together and happy that she just took all of her
rage out on me. She said she never thought of
the consequence until she read in my book
how it impacted me. I felt a lot better after
I read that email, and it allowed me to
look at those bullies in a whole
new light and with some
new compassion."

○ Jessica Weiner ○

author and advice columnist

WE'RE IN COMPETITION ... WITH EACH OTHER

In several studies over the past 10 years, it's been proven that girls are a competitive lot. We compete for looks, popularity, and men. Some scholars think this competitiveness is part of our biological makeup, while others think our strong desire to be the cutest or most popular is due to the high expectations that society places on girls and women (expecting us to be beautiful, sweet, and loving *all* the time). Whatever the reason, each of us aspires on some level to have that Hollywood bod, more friends than Mother Teresa, and the hottest guys on speed dial — and that's a lot to live up to. One of the easiest ways to ensure your rise to the top? Knock down those around you.

CALLING SOMEBODY ELSE FAT WON'T MAKE YOU ANY SKINNIER. CALLING SOMEONE STUPID DOESN'T MAKE YOU ANY SMARTER."

— CADY HERON,
MEAN GIRLS (2004)

Biologically Competitive

This kind of competition rears its ugly head in our romantic lives (in our fights over boys). Some scientists say that women (like men) are biologically primed (also see page 12) to be on the hunt for the strongest, most attractive mate. According to this theory, we may subconsciously try to hurt the reputations of other girls in order to better our own chances. This could explain why girls sling insults like "slut," which can instantly take a girl out of the "respectable mate" category. Of course, many scientists also agree that women, biologically, are capable of forming strong bonds in order to help keep the species alive and thriving. Interestingly, we may be biologically primed to both compete and unite.

"We live in a culture right now that pits girls against each other. We are brought up socially to be in competition with each other—who has the best body, more boyfriends, better clothes. And this kind of competition can be devastating on female friendships because it emphasizes a mentality that there isn't enough to go around. Enough love. Enough attention. Enough success. But there is. There is enough to share with your girlfriends."

° Jessica Weiner °

author and advice columnist

Historically Competitive

Throughout history, women have felt they had to fight to stay on top, even when it came to getting hitched. Back in the day, when marriage was the only way for a girl to leave her parents' home (and it still is in some countries), the prettiest and/or strongest girls were traditionally selected first to get married (suitors paid a higher dowry for women who looked good and/or would be good field-workers and child-bearers). So even sisters competed for mates. Also, a man could have multiple wives, and so the wives battled it out to be considered the favorite and get the best treatment.

Today, the courtship process operates a little differently (thank goodness!), but subtle feelings of competition among girls remain, handed down from earlier generations. Nowadays the competition is often about more complex things: grades, artistic accomplishments, popularity. But it's still there.

"Women and girls are taught that it's not OK to be proud of themselves — that if they talk about what they do well, they will appear 'stuck up.' So, instead of accentuating their positive traits, they accentuate other girls' negative ones, scoring social points not with their own accomplishments, but by honing in on the faults of others."

Kate Izquierdo

music editor, *San Francisco Bay Guardian*

Situationally Competitive

Another interesting point researchers have made is that traditionally there have been fewer males than females on the planet, due to a higher infant mortality rate among boys and also because during wartime many young men have been lost in battle. The result: *many* women trying to land a *few* men. There may be more guys out there nowadays, but when situations of scarcity do arise, women (like men) have a tendency to compete over a potential partner.

Under the Radar

The weird thing about this kind of competition is that we often don't realize we are engaging in it. But we are, even when all we're doing is saying that someone else looks bad in order to feel a little better about ourselves. Realizing that a lot of the bad energy among girls is about competition won't necessarily make it all stop (especially if the others don't realize it), but at least knowing that may make it easier to deal with — and perhaps abstain from.

"The deck is already stacked against us because society conveys the message that we women must be in competition with each other for boyfriends and looks. But if we give in to that theory, nobody wins. Our women friends have great riches to share with us. I am so lucky to have met along the way wonderful women who didn't allow feelings of competition to color my relationship with them and, for that, I am infinitely blessed."

° Mary Jo Pehl °

writer and actor

2

METHODS
of Our
Meanness

*L*ike ninjas, assassins, and vampire slayers, girls have an impressive arsenal of weapons (no one ever said we weren't smart!) that range from subtle to obvious. We use these tricks and techniques to try to damage the confidence, reputations, and overall self-esteem of other girls.

Of course, not all girls are scammers and plotters. Some use these tools intentionally, and others use them subconsciously after falling victim to one or another themselves. Each method of meanness brings a certain result, whether it's a feeling of complete isolation after being ignored or complete paranoia thanks to a sudden betrayal from a trusted friend. While some tools are used one-on-one to cause pain, others are wielded in group situations. Sometimes a good friend will come to your aid. In other situations, bystanders (a boyfriend, a different friend, even a teacher) might see what's happening, yet do nothing to help.

In this chapter, you'll find a breakdown of six of the most common methods of girl-on-girl cruelty; for each method, there's an analysis of why it's used and suggestions regarding how to respond if it's ever used on you. As you read, make a mental note of every time one of these tools has been used against (or by) you. Sometimes just identifying what you've been a victim — or perpetrator — of helps to understand it better.

"No one likes a mean girl. They might fear her for a while, but they will never like her, and they will never, ever honestly respect her."

Hannah Aitchison

tattoo artist and illustrator

SILENT TREATMENT

This is one of the oldest tricks in the book. It basically means that the girl who is angry with you has suddenly gone deaf and blind to your existence. By refusing to answer your questions or even notice you're in the room, it's like she waved a wand and *poof* — you're gone. Um, but you're not gone. You're standing *right* there.

It sounds like a fifth-grade antic, but if you stop and think for a moment, you can probably recall being given this treatment (or its close cousin, the cold shoulder) some time in the last few months. The silent treatment may also involve things like un-returned phone calls and texts. When a girl really does not know how to communicate her feelings *at all*, this is what she does.

> "When you act out against someone in a way that doesn't let them respond to you, it shows them that you are afraid or insecure. Don't do it. It makes you look bad to others, and it makes you feel even worse about yourself."
>
> ❝ **Hannah Aitchison** ❞
> tattoo artist and illustrator

⇒ How It Works

A girl decides that you have done something bad
and must be punished. Instead of having a heart-
to-heart, she successfully puts the brakes on any
two-way conversation. This gets even worse if she's
surrounded by friends who also refuse to make
eye contact with you. Soon the shared lunch table
doesn't have enough seats or your group that gathers
by the lockers before fifth period has moved to
a new location … without leaving a forwarding
address. In the worst cases, you might even walk
into a classroom where your friends are happily
chatting away — then instantly go quiet when you
arrive. Can you say isolation, loneliness, *and* paranoia?

⇒ Why She Does It

Girls usually apply the silent treatment as a severe
but temporary punishment to teach you a lesson
— what life would be like without them. And it's
the type of "punishment" that easily falls below the
radar of the adults in your life because it is so quiet.
For that reason, it also won't garner much sympathy
from teachers and parents — who may even accuse
you of making up the situation in your head! The
girl who uses the silent treatment is the one who
literally does not know how to say how she feels.
So she doesn't.

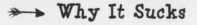

Why It Sucks

First, you feel like a ghost. It's awful to be yelled at, but at least you're not questioning your own existence. Second, you have no control over when the punishment will end. It could last hours, days, weeks, or even months. (If it goes on for longer, it basically falls into the category of Dumping — see page 52). You also have *no* idea what you did wrong because no one is talking (and you can't apologize if no one is listening). You end up a paranoid basket case thinking that the next thing you do or say could make it worse.

What You Can Do

You can attempt to confront the person and ask them what is wrong, but don't try to apologize or grovel — it just gives the user more power. If she continues to ignore you, just go about your business. In most cases, she'll start talking to you again. Then, you need to decide if the friendship is really worth hanging on to.

GOSSIPING

Knowledge is power, sure. After all, school is built on the idea that the more information you can pack into your brain, the better. But that doesn't mean people should excavate dirt on other people and spread it around like the paparazzi do. It doesn't really matter if the dirt being spread is about the head cheerleader, the new guy in school, or that weird kid with the famous uncle. Whatever it is, it's probably only half true and doing damage to someone.

Gossiping always seems like fun — when it's about other people. For instance, it might seem fun to speculate about who's going to get dumped, who's cheating on whom, and who's been plagiarizing Wikipedia entries in her research papers and is about to get kicked out of school. That is, until one of the girls you have been gossiping about finds out. And you can be fairly certain that whoever you are swapping gossip with will eventually dish dirt with someone else … about you.

"If you're hanging out with girls who are being nice to you but practically disowning another friend for showing up late to a party, guess what? They're probably talking about you that way."

○ Lisa Hix ○

magazine writer and Web producer

➤ How It Works

Some gossiping is premeditated, and some isn't. If it's premeditated, the gossiper may play the sympathetic friend when you spill your guts about a big problem like a breakup, family tragedy, or divorce. In reality, she is merely gleaning information from you that she will remember and eventually pass along to others. In other circumstances, you might tell a friend a secret and that girl then mindlessly repeats it to the entire school. Or a girl makes up something about you and blabs it to the entire school and you have to spend the rest of the year denying it.

➤ Why She Does It

Girls, in general, love to bond with each other, and the way we do it (as you might have guessed) is by talking. In that sense, gossiping is a pretty common habit. But girls gossip for reasons other than bonding. Some are jealous or insecure and want to take down peers in order to feel better about themselves; others like to inspire fear in people who know that a gossiper can ruin reputations in a heartbeat; and others simply like to be the center of attention. Sometimes girls who gossip are not trying to be malicious at all but just want acceptance or attention from other girls. Your story — whatever it is — might seem so compelling that the gossiping girl will deem it cool enough to pass along to the immediate universe.

"Most mean girls
are insecure. They're struggling
to control their changing worlds by
implementing a system of domination and
submission in the schoolyard, creating arbitrary
rules for themselves and their peers to follow. The
most important thing is not to buy into it. Five years
down the road, when you're moving forward with
your life and accomplishing your goals, the
gossip and bullying you endured at the
manicured hands of mean girls will
seem inconsequential."

◦ **Meghan Gaynor** ◦

skater, LA Derby Dolls

➻ Why It Sucks

Gossip has often been equated to wildfire because
once it starts spreading, it's very hard to stop it. And
people will judge others they hardly know based on
some story they once heard. We can all probably
think of one person we never became friends
with — whether consciously or subconsciously
— simply because of something someone once
told us. Victims of gossip often walk around with
reputations they did not earn and, sometimes, don't
even know about.

➤ What You Can Do

Protect yourself! Choose your friends very carefully, and tell your deepest secrets only to trusted people who also confide in you. A friend who tells you honestly what is going on in her life is less likely to blab your business all over school than a friend who stays quiet while you let it all out.

> "I think that girls form strong bonds with other girls really quickly, unlike guys who take a while to get to know each other. When girls become friends so fast, they sometimes misjudge the people they choose to hang out with. That's why it is important to establish friendships with people you really trust."
>
> ○ Elizabeth McGrath ○
>
> lead singer for Miss Derringer and visual artist

Of course, not all gossip is even based on truth, and it can be very hard to disprove false allegations that you are a "slut" or have some rare contagious disease. When lies are being passed around about you, the best thing to do is calmly deny them (if anyone asks you) or simply ignore them. If you make a big deal about the rumor or choose to counter-gossip, you can be sure that it will take much longer for people to forget what they heard.

method
3

BOYFRIEND STEALING/ COUPLE SPLITTING

Though not all boys are ready to jump off the couple cruise the minute another girl starts flirting with them, some will. And if it's your best friend doing the flirting, you may end up watching helplessly as she throws Cupid (and you) overboard to get to your guy.

While it's perfectly normal for girls to get into squabbles over Mr. Perfect (who is not really, as everyone learns later, Mr. Perfect), it helps to understand that these squabbles are often less about the guy and more about competition and jealousy.

⟶ How It Works

It can work in many ways, but here's one scenario. Let's say you have a crush, but you're painfully shy. You have three classes with this guy and your lockers are inches apart, but you can't get the nerve up to say hello, let alone ask him on a date.

Your friend says she's more than happy to be the go-between. She offers to talk to him during gym to see what he thinks of you. She'll do all the recon work and you'll reap the benefits. Right? Wrong. Instead of asking him what he thinks of you, she flirts with him and gets his number. You ask what's up, and she says he thinks you're nice and all — but you're just not his type. The next thing you know, she and your crush are going to the prom together.

Or maybe you and your boyfriend are having a big fight over something stupid, and your friend offers to mediate. She starts by listening to both sides, but then she feeds each side lies. She might tell your boyfriend you've been cheating on him for months, or tell you that he's been calling you a prude to his friends. Or perhaps she doesn't lie about anything; she just tells both of you hurtful things the other said or did in moments of anger and trusted you not to share. Either way, her actions break you two apart. She and your beau may not end up together, but neither will you and your beau.

➵➔ Why She Does It

If she stole your guy, she may say (and even think) that she did it because she really liked him. But in most scenarios she and your ex will wind up breaking up shortly afterward. And in some situations, she doesn't even land him in the end. So, why else would she do it?

It's possible that she feels jealous that you are in a relationship and she isn't. If she's your best friend, she might also hate the fact that she's no longer 100 percent responsible for your happiness *or* receiving all of your attention. Or maybe she is one of those girls who need to know she can get any guy in the room, no matter who he is, which means she's insecure about herself — no matter how pretty she may be.

➤ Why It Sucks

The obvious reason it sucks is that a) you just lost your boyfriend and b) you probably just lost your friend, too. This also means you have no one left to gripe about it to. Your parents will have little sympathy when you lose your Prince Charming because they never took the relationship seriously anyway.

➤ What You Can Do

You might think the answer is to never let your friend get near any guy you like, but being distrustful is poisonous to friendships and your relationships. So, there's really not much you can do to avoid this kind of situation. If it ever happens to you, try to understand why your friend did it and that it really had nothing to do with you. And try not to forget that it takes two to tango — meaning the guy was guilty of betrayal as well. And you don't want guys like that in your life anyway.

"We need to
stop stealing each others'
guys. Girls can be very
competitive, and it can be a real
ego boost to get a guy away from
another girl — the idea being that if you
trump that girl, you must be pretty hot stuff.
But it's a completely low thing to do.

"I think the worst thing I ever did to another girl
was knowingly steal her boyfriend. I fell for him pretty
hard and just didn't even think about that girl. Since
then I've really started to feel like women should
all treat each other like sisters (the sister you
love, not the sister you torment).

"We need to help each other
whenever and however we
can, because we all
can use it."

° **Isabel Samaras** °

painter

method 4

VERBAL ABUSE

If you have siblings, you know all too well what it means to be teased. It's bad enough to get that at home, but to get it at school is a nightmare. At the heart of it is good, old-fashioned juvenile name-calling. Other girls will attack you and everything that goes with you: hair, skin, clothes, accent, lisp, intelligence, money, weight, family name, job, religion, sexual orientation, you name it. They don't think anything of it, but verbal abuse like this can totally wreck your self-confidence.

Name-callers sometimes claim they were only joking, and they may even tell you to lighten up. But if they really care about you, they should know when they've gone too far and the joke is on you. They may say they were laughing *with* you, not *at* you. Only you weren't laughing.

How It Works

In some situations, a girl finds your weak point—your nose, braces, acne, stutter, height—and then makes a catchy and degrading nickname that stays with you forever. Every time she calls you the nickname instead of your real name it completely deflates your ego. Other times, girls just say really hurtful things that have no truth to them at all.

A super-destructive example of teasing is also known as "slut-bashing." Sexually explicit nicknames can ruin reputations, turning virginal classmates into virtual porn stars overnight. If you get called a slut at school, it may have zero to do with sex. Perhaps it's because you are pretty or wear revealing clothes or none of the above. Many girls use the word as an all-purpose insult. And despite the fact that society has totally over-sexualized girls and that most female celebrities are hailed for dressing promiscuously, getting called a slut is not going to make you rich and famous — it's more likely to ruin your reputation.

➤ Why She Does It

Many name-callers and other verbal abusers have had to deal with endless teasing from family members, and so they've come to believe it's normal to belittle friends and kids they don't even know. They may just be doing it to you because it was done to them.

Others do it to protect themselves: Pointing out your perceived flaws gives a teaser a false sense of security (that her own imperfections will be overlooked if everyone else is distracted by yours). Sometimes, name-calling is simply used to gain power in a small social circle or on campus in general.

Why It Sucks

The worst part about being verbally abused by peers is that — even if they call you names that have nothing to do with who you are — *you* may start to believe that what they're saying is true. And if they call you things like slut or whore, *others* may begin to believe it is true. And what if girls are picking on things that *are* true about you (like your height, weight, or race)? Then, you start to believe that there must be something wrong with those things even when there clearly isn't.

What You Can Do

Because most of us don't ever want to look like a crybaby or a humorless drone, you may try to tolerate the joke. But everyone has a limit. If the comments are coming from a friend, approach her when she's not teasing you and tell her how you feel about it. If she doesn't stop, you might want to reconsider whether the friendship is worth it. If the comments are coming from a stranger, try to ignore her. Sometimes people stop when they don't get a reaction.

Hate Crimes

In some states, it is considered a hate crime to call someone a name that is ethnically insulting, racist, sexist, or homophobic. Know your rights and report serious verbal abuse to authorities.

"Girls have always had cliques and hierarchies; they have always gossiped and bitched and ostracized each other. It's nothing new. I've learned that, as a society, we denote women who hate other women as 'strong.' In reality, they're not strong at all. They're actually quite weak."

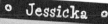 **Jessicka**

vocalist, Jack Off Jill and Scarling.

"One of the best ways I learned to cope was to ignore it. It sounds hard and it sounds weak. But I was able to really ice these girls out, and soon they grew bored of me."

 **Jessica Weiner**

author and advice columnist

CYBER ABUSE

Thanks to the Internet and cell phones, it's a brave new wired world … of vindictive girls lurking out in cyberspace. The web is the perfect place for people to unleash their meanness because it is fast, easy, public, and potentially anonymous. In the old days, girls used journals called slam books, in which they would write what they hated about each other and pass it around; today they simply post their comments on MySpace or Facebook pages for all the world to see.

➻ How It Works

The ways to cyberbully are endless. People can send degrading emails, post mean comments on someone's social networking page, and even forward a personal confession from a trusting confidant to the entire 10th grade. Some girls even make fake profiles or URL pages solely to tease, mock, and humiliate another person.

Another form of cyber abuse is identity theft. Although another girl can't use your credit card number to charge a year's worth of clothes (because presumably you don't have a credit card yet), she can take your contact info and photo (or, worse, Photoshop your head onto a naked girl's body) and sign you up for a free trial of an online dating service. Before you know it, your inbox has been inundated with creepy emails and porn spam. Or, if someone knows your IM screen name and password, she can secretly log on pretending to be you and pick fights with other girls or proposition guys.

> "High school was tough, but I could at least leave it at school in the hallway. Now, girls come home, hop on their computers, and get hazed through IM and email. I don't even want to think of what my life would have been like if girls back then had had access to technology the way they do now."
>
> **Jessica Weiner**
> author and advice columnist

➺→ Why She Does It

It's way easier to say mean stuff online than to someone's face, so girls who are unable to communicate maturely will go for your throat by going to the keyboard. And it's hard for them to get caught because most parents don't understand online culture and don't see what's happening. Cyber abuse can also be seen as a game or a group activity. Some uninspired girls think it's entertaining to get together and spend an evening ripping apart another girl online.

➻ Why It Sucks

It sucks mainly because it is so public and spreads so fast. It used to be that a kid could pass a mean note around class, and 20 or 30 people would eventually know what it said. With cyberspace, a click of a button means thousands or even millions of people instantly have dirt on you. The anonymity factor only makes it worse because when you don't know who is behind such cruelty, you become paranoid about why some-one would say such awful things and find yourself wondering how to protect or defend yourself.

➻ What You Can Do

Unless you think you might be in danger, the best thing to do is to not do anything. Getting into a catty cyberwar will only make things worse and give her the satisfaction that she upset you. Plus, she'll have evidence that you participated in the problem, should you ever want to report her.

Other solutions:

- Block or delete the person from your profile, IM buddy list, and blog.

- Don't install applications on social networking sites that allow people to post anonymous stuff on your page.

- Contact customer support for the site and get them to locate and shut down the offenders.

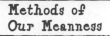

- If the abuse is taking place on campus, let your school know. Lots of schools are beginning to have policies against cyber abuse.

- If it gets really bad, take legal action. See pages 74–75 to find out what to do.

Protect Your Password

One of the best things you can do to protect yourself in cyberspace is to be password smart. Do NOT use the same password for every site. It's devastating enough if someone figures out (or shares) your password for your social networking profile, but if you used the same password for your MP3 music service and your email account, you could end up with anything from false charges to embarrassing disclosures of personal information.

Some other tips:

- If someone breaks into any of your accounts, change your password ASAP (or delete your account and create a new one, if possible).

- Even if no one breaks in, make a habit of changing your passwords regularly to prevent hackers from gaining access.

- Do not share or write down your passwords.

DUMPING

We all know how heartbreaking it is when some guy we're dating suddenly stops calling or coming around. The same heartbreaking feeling takes over when a best friend decides one day that she's no longer interested in hanging out.

➤ How It Works

If your friend has any courage at all, she tells you to your face that she no longer wants to be friends and why. But in most scenarios, she is suddenly "too busy" to hang out, talk on the phone, or text. She can't go to the movies because her mom needs her for something vague. Or she has to walk the dog — a lot and alone. You're getting blown off, and the more you try to hang on to the friendship the more you seem to drive her away.

➤ Why It Sucks

You feel betrayed and lonely. This is your go-to person on *everything*. Your confidant. Your sidekick. Because of all of this, getting dumped by a best friend can be worse than getting dumped by a boyfriend. And if she doesn't even tell you why, it's unsettling and confusing; she's acting as if your friendship never existed — but you still have all of the photos, emails, and memories to prove that it did.

➤ Why She Does It

Maybe she wants to climb the social ladder and feels like you're holding her back. Or perhaps she just wants to join a new group of friends and not have to automatically add you to the new entourage, or change her persona overnight without keeping you around as a reminder of who she used to be. Some girls and women never know the real reason why that best friend just wrote them off, either because the friend was unable to communicate it or because the friend herself never really understood why she did it.

➤ What You Can Do

It's hard to know how to behave when this happens to you. When you get dumped in a romantic relationship, you get to wallow in self-pity and watch sad movies. Your friends sympathize with you and say he was a jerk anyway. But this is different. A friend doesn't ever really promise you faithfulness (the way a guy might), so it can be hard to blame her if she just starts hanging out with other people. And if you cry and beg too much, you only feel worse. Sometimes it's best to just recognize that many friendships come and go, and this is one of them. Even if your heart hurts, try to move on; just as with romantic relationships, you will feel better when you meet someone else.

3
BEARING
the Brunt
of It

Everyone feels — at one point or another — like they are getting dealt more grief than they deserve from their friends and peers. Maybe you get ousted from your group for no reason, or maybe you become an Internet celebrity overnight in a way that's less than positive. If you are suffering at the hands of girl-inflicted cruelty, you're probably not in a happy place.

Parents and teachers may tell you to just ignore it and it'll go away. That might work for zits, but you'd have to be a Zen master to completely tune out those annoying whispers, evil-eye glares, and snide comments. Besides, by pretending it's not happening, you're actually denying yourself the right to be angry. And ignoring how you really feel has the potential to make you feel worse.

While there are specific ways to handle certain
situations (discussed in the previous chapter),
there are also some general coping strategies
and communication tactics for dealing with
difficult girls and difficult situations.

"My mom was
always telling me all that
'This too shall pass' kinda stuff,
which turned out to be 100 percent true
but is absolutely meaningless when you're
right in the middle of it. Who cares if it
will be in the past someday?
I'm in this shit NOW!"

° Isabel Samaras °

painter

strategy 1

KEEP YOUR COOL

There is a communication philosophy called "Respond, don't react." The idea is that you take in what is being said to you and then calmly respond to it, rather than react in a wild frenzy. Sometimes you may feel like screaming and yelling, but the more you yell, the angrier you get, which only hurts you. Besides, harassers actually *enjoy* watching their victims fly into a rage. It's amusing — like watching an angry little video game.

If you can take it, let the other person endlessly rant and rave. Listen patiently without interrupting. Soon enough she will tire out and wonder why you're not responding in kind. (The same is true if you get an angry email.)

The idea is that you don't take the bait. You allow the frantic girl to vent and then you respond rationally. Staying calm keeps your heart rate down and your ability to think intact. It may not always stop someone from harassing you, but it will prevent her from getting the best of you.

MASTERING OTHERS IS STRENGTH.
MASTERING YOURSELF IS TRUE POWER."
—TAO TE CHING

"By maintaining that calm-but-strong attitude, you retain your dignity and make them realize that you're not going home and obsessing about them the way they clearly are doing about you!"

Alexandra Tyler

writer and performer, The Devil-Ettes

CONFRONT HER

Nobody likes to deal with head-on conflict, except maybe prizefighters and crash test dummies, so it's not a shocker that entering into a screaming match with the girl who told everyone that you've had sex with the entire football team isn't on your to-do list. However, instead of the usual strategy of talking behind her back to form alliances with other girls, why not just … talk to her?

Calmly confronting someone who has hurt you is not the easiest thing, but it's definitely the most mature. Here are some tips for your encounter:

1. Talk to her in person.

Text and email might seem less intimidating, but those methods are a poor replacement for face-to-face conversation. Besides, the issue might be a touchy one and you don't want to find a transcript of your entire fight online somewhere.

2. Talk to her without an audience.

Try to talk to her when no one else is around. She is more likely to hear what you have to say when she is not distracted by or trying to impress other people.

3. Tell her specifically why you are hurt.

Cite examples. Try to be direct but don't get aggressive or overly accusatory. Just make your point and be clear.

4. Prepare.

Write down everything you want to say in a letter first, then look it over before going to talk to her. Of course, conversations never go quite as planned, but at least you'll have a plan, and you'll be less likely to get sidetracked by some petty point she brings up. Or you could also act out the conversation with a trusted friend. Say everything that's on your mind and have your friend say things you think the girl you're confronting might say. See if you can stay calm and focused even if she gets agitated. This will give you more confidence to go through with it and reduce the chances of not saying everything you'd hoped to.

> "Putting yourself out there in the name of truth can be disarming to the other party, and it makes you feel like you stood up for yourself and you cared enough about yourself to face it head-on."
>
> **Mary Jo Pehl**
> writer and actor

strategy

3

FORGIVE

Just ended a long fight with a friend? After you clear
the air, let the incident go. Sometimes we fall into the
nasty trap of holding a grudge. We say we've forgiven
the people who have wronged us but then remember
every bad thing our friends (and boyfriends, parents,
siblings, and teachers) have ever done and bring it
up again during every fight. By doing this, we're not
really *forgiving* them. If you look up "forgiveness" in
most dictionaries, it says something like "the process
of ceasing to feel resentment, indignation, or anger
against another person for a perceived offence." In
other words, when you forgive a friend you can't
continue to be angry about what she did and still
want her to suffer for it.

That, of course, doesn't mean you should let people
treat you badly. If someone continually treats you
like crap, your self-esteem will be sure to suffer. In
these cases, it may be time to cut these so-called
friends loose (see page 64).

"LISA SIMPSON: **BUT I'M SO ANGRY.**

MARGE SIMPSON: **YOU'RE A WOMAN.
YOU CAN HOLD ON TO IT FOREVER."**

—*THE SIMPSONS MOVIE* (JULY 2007)

"In high school,
a close friend left me at a
party to leave with a guy. I was very
upset and got a ride home, but we talked
about it the next day and worked it out. Since
I never had a boyfriend in high school and my
best friend did, after this incident she started
including me in the things they did together.
She ended up going above and beyond
what is expected in a friendship. We
are still friends to this day."

Jenny Conlee

keyboardist, The Decemberists

strategy
4

CUT TIES

No one likes to be called a quitter, but sometimes you need to cut your losses. When you have given 100 percent to a friendship but just can't make it work, you have to call it quits. It's hard to do, but think about all the times this person may have lied to you, gossiped about you, or hurt you in some other way. This friend doesn't have your best interests at heart, and it's starting to seem like the longer you hold on to this friendship, the worse your life gets.

Though it's difficult, telling her in person is the most mature way to sever the friendship. Be compassionate and calm, but make it clear that you've been hurt enough and can't continue to be friends at this time. It can do wonders for your self-esteem when you finally stand up for yourself and let people know that you refuse to be treated like a second-class friend. The friendship may even start up again later and be stronger for the time spent apart.

"Don't make space in
your head for people who make
you miserable. And if one of your friends
turns out to be one of those people? You might
not have space in your life anymore for them
either! Give 'em a chance for redemption, but
don't let anyone keep screwing you over
or hurting you repeatedly."

Isabel Samaras

painter

"I do NOT allow
myself to be mistreated.
I step up now and tell it like it is.
Took my whole life to get here,
but it feels good!"

Jane Wiedlin

founding member, The Go-Go's

GET IT OUT OF YOUR SYSTEM

Being on the receiving end of constant harassment is stressful; sometimes you simply need to vent. If you don't, it will eat at you and maybe even make you physically ill.

Here are three ways to let off some steam:

1. Write in a journal.

This is a great way to get all that worry-wart junk out of your brain and on to paper. (Just make sure your journal is well hidden.)

2. Do something physical, like run, kickbox, or practice yoga.

Exercise is one of the best ways to make yourself feel better because it decreases the levels of stress hormones in your body and increases the production of serotonin and endorphins, which boost your mood. The result is that awesome exercise high.

3. Talk it out.

Gabbing with a pal can be a great way to de-stress. Have a marathon conversation with a friend who lives in a different state, knows none of the people you know, has a sympathetic ear, and can make you laugh. (Laughing also lowers levels of stress hormones in the body.)

"Sometimes things seem much worse simply because we're tired or mentally drained. Taking a break and remembering to keep your sense of humor can really help. Don't bottle up your frustration —get it out. Start a band, photograph it, paint it, or write it all down so you can read it later in order to remember how far you've come. This time of frustration will pass. People will grow and change, and sometimes the people who taunt you the most may not matter or won't be around a year from now."

o Jessicka o

vocalist, Jack Off Jill and Scarling.

strategy
6

BREAK OUT

Spending your waking hours taking notes, roaming from class to class, and simply dwelling behind the walls and windows of that chaotic structure otherwise known as "school" may be your typical routine, but does that mean all of your friends must come from that building? Hardly. If you have really tried to make things work but keep getting shut down by the snobby girls who strut down your high school's hallways like they're on a never-ending catwalk, then it's time to branch out.

Believe it or not, there's a whole social world outside the gates of your great (or maybe not so great) educational institution. Some ideas are:

○ start a club

○ volunteer at a teen center

○ attend an all-girls surf or rock camp

○ take an art class at the local community college

By searching outside your usual crowd and trying
different things, you'll meet new people who just
might end up being your closest friends. And by
pursuing things you are passionate about, you'll find
a safe environment in which to express yourself *and*
a place where people judge you a whole lot less.

*"I think of the
time I spent as a teen
gossiping with all my friends, and
I wish I had that time now to do
something creative with."*

⊙ Elizabeth McGrath ⊙

lead singer for Miss Derringer and visual artist

*"The more I started
to think about myself and what
I was interested in, the less I cared
about the other morons. I had my little
group of friends, my music, and my art,
and the other stuff just started
to fade away."*

⊙ Isabel Samaras ⊙

painter

4
CALLING
in
Reinforcements

hile there is a lot you can do to manage difficult situations on your own, there are times when you really do need help from the outside — from parents, teachers, counselors, coaches, big sisters, or anyone who can step in if things get dangerous.

Sure, you may avoid telling anyone about what's going on because you are embarrassed, proud, or afraid the problem will only escalate with parental involvement. But when things get really bad, you obviously need to do something about it. If you are dealing with any of the situations on the following pages, make a decision to call in reinforcements.

"There are too many instances where abuse goes unreported or unpunished because a girl feels afraid to speak up. But that's like saying it's OK and she somehow deserves what is happening to her. That's ridiculous! Why shouldn't someone have consequences for their actions?

"If someone steals, they go to jail; if they lie, they get called out; and if they hurt someone, they should be held accountable for that as well."

Hannah Aitchison

tattoo artist and illustrator

YOU'RE RECEIVING THREATS ONLINE

It's one thing when you get obnoxious emails from friends or random girls at school, or if someone keeps posting stupid comments on your MySpace or Facebook page. It's annoying, and even potentially depressing, but your ego is probably more in danger than anything else.

But what happens when it goes further than that? Maybe someone posts a comment on your blog telling you to expect a beatdown if you show your face at school the next day. Or you get emailed a death threat. Cyber abuse is actually kind of scary when taken to this level. You can't simply ignore or delete a message that challenges your personal safety. This is serious stuff. You've got to tell your parents, and you may even want to go to the police.

In situations like this, it's important to keep proof of all interactions. Print out copies of any emails, profile comments, instant messages, and/or text messages to show as evidence. (Even though you may want to hit the Delete key the second you get a nasty note, don't. Save the note instead.) If someone calls you and leaves a threatening message, save it. Then, record it onto your computer if you have a program that allows you to do that. The more proof you have, the easier it is for the police to take action. Law enforcement agencies are surprisingly savvy when it comes to cyber crime and harassment, but you need to help them as much as you can.

What's Really Happening Online

42% of kids have been harassed online

35% of kids have been threatened online

53% of kids admit having said something mean or hurtful to another person online

58% of kids have not told their parents or an adult about something mean or hurtful that happened to them online

(According to i-SAFE, an Internet safety organization.)

YOU'RE GETTING HAZED

If you're getting emotionally or physically abused by a group of girls as part of some traditional initiation process, you're being hazed. A form of group-enforced peer pressure in which you are expected to follow orders without question, hazing (though called different things at different times) has been around for ages. College sororities may use it to determine which pledges care more about the sisterhood than their own personal comfort. High school cheerleading squads and sports teams often use it as a way of getting members into shape and, at the same time, initiating them. And many schools have an unspoken tradition of upperclassmen hazing younger students as a rite of passage (ever hear of Freshman Friday?).

Hazing is a favorite among girls in high school because it has the power to mess with your mind. You may think you're not getting hazed when, in fact, you are. Being asked to do things that make you feel degraded or small is a good tip-off. Are the new girls you're hanging out with always making you illegally buy alcohol for them at the corner store with someone else's fake ID? Do the older girls on your team or squad ask you (and other newbies) to do unnecessary things like run in the rain on freezing cold days or kiss boys you don't know when out at parties? That's all hazing. And it can get worse.

For instance, some cliques test wannabe members by making them guzzle beer until they puke or have sex with total strangers. This is dangerous stuff. And though some power-trippers claim that these rituals help form bonds among those who participate, let's face it: There are lots of other, more effective ways to bond.

Running with the popular crowd might as well be like running with the bulls in Spain. It's thrilling at first — and then you get impaled with a bullhorn. The bottom line is that no group that would purposely put its members in danger is worth joining. Not sure how to distinguish between group bonding and hazing? Ask yourself this question: Is this activity hurting me physically or emotionally? If the answer is yes, it's hazing. If you feel like you're being hazed — or like you're being pressured to haze other people — do whatever you need to do to remove yourself from the situation.

History of Hazing

Hazing in high school is not new. In fact, back in the '70s, it was often a formal daylong event in which the upperclassmen would make the lower classmen do things like crawl on all fours in the mud or get egged in their underwear. Nowadays most schools have banned hazing, but it still goes on under the radar.

scenario 3

YOU'RE BEING PHYSICALLY THREATENED OR ABUSED

Most of the cruelty girls face in high school — and beyond — is of the mental or emotional kind (which is what this book has mainly been talking about). But not all girls are passive-aggressive. In fact, some are seriously aggressive-aggressive. You can use a lot of peaceful tactics when you are getting messed with mentally, but what do you do if you're getting pummeled? While openly expressing anger is healthier than suppressing feelings, that's no excuse for one girl to use another girl as a punching bag.

The best thing to do is to tell an adult you trust — and who won't overreact. (If your mom approaches the attacker at school, and yells at her in front of everyone, it's not going to make your life any better.) The person you talk to should know the proper channels to go through to get you out of danger. If you are getting beaten up badly, or are being threatened or attacked with weapons, go to the police immediately. Too many girls think they can handle stuff on their own when they can't, and they wind up hospitalized or worse because of pride. An adult would get help if she were in danger — you should, too.

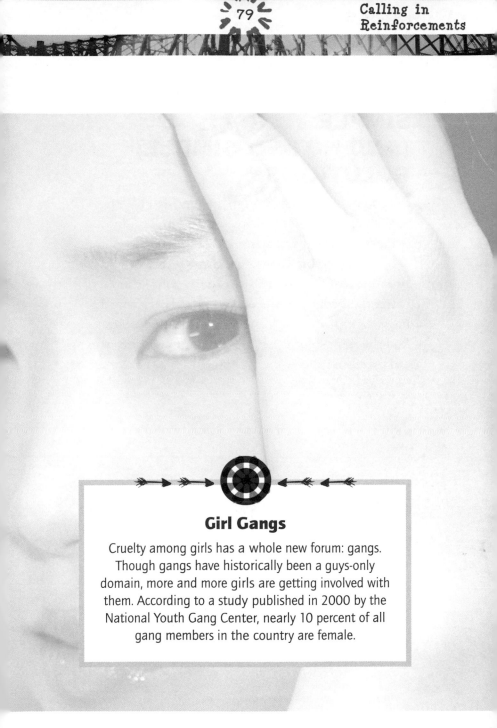

Girl Gangs

Cruelty among girls has a whole new forum: gangs.
Though gangs have historically been a guys-only
domain, more and more girls are getting involved with
them. According to a study published in 2000 by the
National Youth Gang Center, nearly 10 percent of all
gang members in the country are female.

SIMPLE (AND NOT-SO-SIMPLE) SOLUTIONS

So, you've finally had enough and decided to get some help from outside forces. Good move. Now you need to figure out what kind of help you will ask for. Remember that you know the details of the situation *and* the social landscape of your school better than your parents or teachers. That's why it's important that you ask them to work *with* you to find the right solution. Here are some solutions you can propose.

"It's important to get the school involved because you might not be the only one a particular person is harassing, and the school can address the problem in a much bigger and more far-reaching way that might help others, as well."

Hannah Aitchison

tattoo artist and illustrator

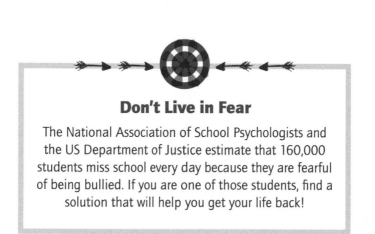

Don't Live in Fear

The National Association of School Psychologists and the US Department of Justice estimate that 160,000 students miss school every day because they are fearful of being bullied. If you are one of those students, find a solution that will help you get your life back!

1. Mediation

You obviously don't want to be alone with the girl who is making your life hell, but you can ask a school counselor or a third party to mediate a conversation between you. This can be really illuminating, as you may find out why she is doing what she is doing and will maybe even reach a solution. Alternatively, the mediator could bring in your parents and the other person's parents and mediate among them to try to settle the dispute. Involving a third person will help both sides feel more secure that they are being treated fairly — and guarantee that everyone involved stays safe for the duration of the meeting.

2. Change Your Schedule

If you're sick at the thought of walking or bussing to school every morning because of some abuse you are enduring en route, or if you are getting harassed in the same class every day, the easiest solution might be to change your schedule. Talk with your parents about this. Maybe one of them can drop you off and pick you up, at least until these girls forget about you. Or ask to have your schedule modified so that you don't share classes with the girls who have made it their goal in life to make your life hell.

3. Switch Schools

If the teacher-parent intervention isn't doing the trick and if changing your schedule has not helped, cut your losses and change schools. It might seem drastic, but for all you know, the school on the other side of town could be full of kids who don't pull the same lame crap your current classmates do.

Get Your School Involved

If girl-on-girl cruelty is a big issue in your school, take it
on as a cause. Whether you are a victim yourself,
or are just an observer, you can campaign to
put an end to this viciousness in your school.
Things you can do:

○ Ask the school board to update its policies on
unacceptable and expellable behavior.

○ Organize a day of workshops at school about
girl-on-girl cruelty and how to deal with it.

○ Conduct a seminar on cyber abuse and teach girls
how to protect themselves online.

○ Promote girl unity for your generation by teaching
girls to band together instead of break each
other down (see Chapter 6 for more).

GIRL AGAINST HERSELF

When you are constantly under attack, it may seem like you have no control over your life. In an attempt to feel more powerful, girls sometimes get the urge to mess with the only thing they *can* control — their bodies. Some girls resort to cutting (making actual cuts on one's body with things like razors, scissors, knives, and glass); others go to the extreme with their diets (starving themselves as anorexics do, or binging and purging like bulimics), which can have side effects like anemia, hair loss, and the end to monthly periods — and can even be fatal.

Why do we do this stuff to ourselves when we are being harassed? There are so many reasons, but three top ones are:

○ to distract ourselves from the emotional pain we are feeling

○ to punish ourselves for being who we are (which we think is not good enough)

○ to gain some sense of control over a seemingly desperate situation

Some girls even contemplate suicide because they reason that it's better than facing their tormentors another day. The National Institute of Mental Health reports that as many as 25 suicides are attempted for each one that is completed, and that teen girls are more likely than teen boys to attempt suicide.

The cruel girls in your life are doing enough damage to you already — you certainly don't need to help them. If you are even thinking about harming yourself in any way, find someone you can trust and talk to them. If you don't know where to start, see the numbers and websites on the next page.

Not to Be Taken Lightly

Sticks and stones might break bones, but words never hurt, right? Wrong. Studies have shown that there is a connection between relational aggression — which includes giving the silent treatment, name-calling, gossiping, and cyberbullying — and suicide. Reports in Scandinavia, Japan, and here in the US have confirmed this link.

Places to Contact for Help

SAFE (Self-Abuse Finally Ends)
1-800-DONT-CUT
www.selfinjury.com

National Suicide Prevention Lifeline
1-800-273-TALK
www.suicidepreventionlifeline.org

National Runaway Switchboard
1-800-RUNAWAY
www.1800runaway.org

National Eating Disorders Association
1-800-931-2237
www.myneda.org

*"It may feel like
forever today, but train your
brain to look toward the future.
I thought life was completely pointless when
I was 16, but by the age of 23 I was in the
biggest rock group in America. Had I known what
the future would hold, I would have been a
much happier teen. Have faith that there
are good things ahead for you
that you can create!"*

° Jane Wiedlin °

founding member, The Go-Go's

5
STOPPING
the
Cycle

The media loves to portray things as good and evil. Expressions like "mean girls" and "nice girls" or "bullies" and "victims" give us the idea that half of us is one way and the rest of us another. But it's not so black and white. Most "mean girls" have also been victims in some way, and many "nice girls" can be mean to friends without even realizing it. In order to stop the cycle of girl cruelty, everyone must be willing to take a closer look at themselves and how they treat others.

When we are in a hostile social environment, it can be tricky to know how to be the good guy — or girl. While society spends a lot of time telling us how to defend ourselves against people who do us wrong, we rarely get any good advice on how to keep some of our own bad behavior in check. On the following pages you'll find some tips to help you better understand your own behavior so you can prevent yourself from becoming the bad girl.

"The last thing we need are more women with low self-esteem who feel alienated. We need to learn to empower each other even if it's one girl at a time. The problem is far from new, and the solution isn't a big mystery. We just need to face up to our individual roles in the process."

○ Jessicka ○

vocalist, Jack Off Jill and Scarling.

UNDERSTAND WHY YOU ARE PISSED

Understanding why you are upset is a key part of processing your anger in a healthy way and not exploding at an innocent friend, which only perpetuates the cycle of girl-to-girl bitchiness.

Are you irate because your best friend constantly "forgets" to invite you to her parties, or are you pissed because she spilled the confidential details of your last date to half the junior class? Or are you really just mad because you swore to yourself you'd lose 10 pounds by December and it didn't happen?

Make a list of the reasons why you're angry and be specific. It helps to see all your grievances on paper so you can uncover exactly why you're freaking out. It could be trivial or something deeper. You may even just be in a bad mood.

"We all have the capacity to be mean and hurt others and have all treated someone poorly at some point in our lives, maybe even a sibling. When girls are mean, it's usually because they aren't feeling great about themselves deep down or there are other issues going on at home that they feel powerless over. So being mean to another girl is a way to feel like you have control over at least one part of your life."

Anastasia Goodstein

teen culture expert and author

"I think we need to explore why we feel more comfortable picking on our girlfriends rather than dealing with what's really going on."

Tegan

bandmember, Tegan and Sara

tip 2

LEARN HOW TO COMMUNICATE

A lot of the problems that this book has been talking about are a direct result of lack of communication. Has someone stopped speaking to you?

She doesn't know how to say what is on her mind. Is someone teasing you? She doesn't know how to communicate with you and tell you why she is really upset or even threatened by you. We all need to learn how to communicate more effectively so we can avoid this type of nonsense. Here are three great principles of communication:

1. Don't hold things in.

If a friend hurts you, tell her calmly why you are hurt and then offer to listen to her side of the story. The more you stifle stuff, the more chance there is of you blowing up at someone unintentionally.

"Lack of communication is what causes misunderstandings. Don't expect your friends to be mind readers. If you need to say something to your friend, say it and say it with tact."

Kim Shattuck

lead singer, The Muffs

2. Learn how to listen.

When a friend comes to you with a problem, the first instinct may be to get defensive. Instead, make an effort to really hear what she is saying instead of thinking about what you are going to say next or interrupting her to make a point. Sometimes just having you hear why she is upset is enough to make the problem go away.

3. Move forward.

Ask what you can do to make things better between the two of you. Understand that something might be wrong in the friendship, and together you guys can find a way to rectify it.

"Whenever I can, I try to talk to the person who has been doing hurtful things to me, to approach them in a way in which I can show them I'm not really that different from them. It's a real relief and leads to a feeling of human connection. It's so much better to connect with other girls rather than push them away."

Hannah Aitchison

tattoo artist and illustrator

LEARN TO ADMIT FAULT

When you and your friend have had a fight, it may be hard to see that you are partially to blame. But the truth is that most of us are at least partially wrong for every fight, and the mature thing to do is to admit it — even if you are merely sorry that you unintentionally hurt your friend.

If you decide to take the high road, be sincere. Nothing adds more fuel to the fire than an insincere apology. Saying you're sorry with a shrug of the shoulders and a cold tone is just going to show how much you *don't* care about your friend's feelings. You don't have to beg and grovel, just look her in the eye and tell her you're sorry and mean it. And then talk about ways you can improve your communication, and friendship in general, going forward.

Mutual apologizing after a fight can do wonders in stopping the cycle of cruelty between girls because it puts everyone on an equal playing ground: calm, forgiving, and ready to start over. Of course, if you find yourself always being the first (or only one) to apologize, you might want to take a closer look at the situation. Always taking the blame just to soothe someone's temper won't solve any problems in the long run.

"I am certainly not all 'sugar and spice,' and never have been. I have been a bitch and will be a bitch again some time in the not-so-distant future. I have made mistakes and have grown from them. Sadly, most women have experienced betrayal at the hands of another female. But my hope is that even the 'meanest girl' will become the best she can be when given the room to grow and change."

Jessicka

vocalist, Jack Off Jill and Scarling.

"If I find myself in a situation where some aspect of my behavior seems to keep rubbing all of my friends the wrong way, I try to look honestly at my behavior and do what I can to change it."

Kim Shattuck

lead singer, The Muffs

tip
4

STOP THE BUZZ

If you are one of those girls who claims that you never gossip … you are probably kidding yourself. At one point or another, pretty much everyone gossips — especially girls, since we are such great orators. But while it might be tempting to chat with Susan in world geography class about some melt-down Emma had, and then tell Kristen at lunch and Angela at band practice (before going home and blogging about it), the best thing you can do is let the trail end with you.

It's hard to completely avoid gossip — it's everywhere. But that doesn't mean you have to pick it up, add to it, and spread it around to everyone you know.

"I think the worst thing I have done is talked about another girl behind her back. I always feel so guilty about it. I even lose sleep over it. In the end I get so stressed out about it that I have to tell the person what I said, which makes me look foolish and bitchy to the people around me, and like a freak to the person I talked about! It's easy to get caught up in rumors, but it takes a strong person to avoid the gossip mills."

○ **Elizabeth McGrath** ○

lead singer for Miss Derringer and visual artist

The quickest way to end gossip is to not repeat it. If enough people refuse to keep it going, it fizzles. Sure, that won't get rid of gossip permanently, but at least you'll no longer be a part of its destructive lifecycle. The next time you feel an urge to spread the news, stop and think how it would feel if you were the headline. Physically bite your tongue, snap a rubber band around your wrist, or simply blab it to someone in another state who will never know any of the people you are talking about. Gossiping is a hard habit to break, but it's necessary to stop if you don't want to, even accidentally, cause a lot of pain and suffering to others.

"I wish I could say I never gossiped about another girl, but that isn't true. I stooped to the level of gossip and rumor spreading as a teen to fit in, and while I don't know directly if I ever hurt anyone with my words, I feel badly because I was definitely a part of bad-mouthing certain girls and probably saying things that weren't true about them. Now, as an adult, I really try to not spread rumors or say hurtful things behind my friends' backs. I have learned how to have healthy confrontations, which is important."

Jessica Weiner

author and advice columnist

DON'T PLOT OUT REVENGE

When you're under attack it's tempting to scream "War!" In fact, your first reaction to teasing might be to tease right back —"You think *I'm* fat? *You're* so fat you have to beep when you back up!" Someone texts you a nasty message 30 times, you text them back something worse 60 times. Yup. This could go back and forth forever.

It might sound like a good idea at the time — to make someone pay for what they did to you — but revenge is about the best way to perpetuate, and even escalate, cycles of meanness. Plus, it never really changes what happened. Joanne stole your boyfriend, so you call her mother and reveal where Joanne has really been hanging out on Wednesdays after school. Joanne gets grounded, sure. But you are still alone. It is much better to just accept that you're feeling angry, rejected, alone, or whatever, and then move on.

If you're dead set on revenge, the ideal tactic is to be a better person. As hokey as that sounds, it's true. That fleeting feeling of vindication certainly won't help you achieve the dreams and goals your harasser was trying to sabotage.

"Being yourself
is the
best revenge."

◊ Lynn Peril ◊

author of *Pink Think*

<table>
<tr><td>tip
6</td></tr>
</table>

GET FAMILIAR WITH YOUR EXCUSES

It's easy to see when other girls are acting uncool, but it's harder to identify that kind of behavior in ourselves. When we do mean things to other girls, we usually justify it somehow. If we can recognize our excuses, we can come to see them for what they are: excuses. Ever hear your inner voice saying one of the below?

1. "She deserved it."

Sometimes we look at another girl and, for whatever reason, think she deserves to be the recipient of our unleashed aggression. Maybe she is overweight, younger, dresses provocatively, or is going out with some guy we like. So, we tease her, ignore her, or laugh when we hear dirt spread about her. It might seem harmless, but it's not fair to judge other people that way, and it only perpetuates a cycle of disrespect.

2. "Everyone else is doing it."

You may think you're Miss Independent, but as soon as your pals get together and begin dissecting every tiny detail about the new girl in class, do you chime in or shut them up? If you go along with your friends even when you don't agree with them, you're no longer really in control of who you are. And in this situation, you are likely doing emotional damage to another person. Voice your opinion about why it's wrong — you might actually uncover some allies.

3. "There's no choice."

Maybe you think you need to step on people every once in a while to puff up your social status, win a school election, or compete over a guy. So, you say to yourself, "Well, I really had no choice." But you always have a choice, and you'll never regret making the right decision (though people often regret making the wrong one).

4. "Revenge is only fair."

Being angry is human. And the more you're wronged, the more you feel like drafting elaborate plans of vengeance as you quietly mutter to yourself, "No one does that to me and gets away with it!" But just like physical abuse, emotional abuse is a cycle, and if someone doesn't break the cycle, things will only continue to get worse for everyone involved.

AN EYE FOR AN EYE MAKES
THE WHOLE WORLD BLIND."

— MAHATMA GANDHI

6

TEAMING UP

Instead of

Tearing Each Other Down

o, OK, we know we're not perfect. But to say all girls have no choice but to be catty and mean isn't true. We're not inherently a wicked mob of fashion zombies who can't tell right from wrong.

In fact, a lot of the cruel things we do are just a result of us using our best traits in the wrong ways. Girls are typically great speakers and writers, and we can use that advantage to advocate for people less fortunate than us or to make great works of art instead of gossiping and spreading rumors. We love forming communities, and we can use that to draw *all* people together instead of creating exclusive cliques. We are the more emotionally tuned-in gender, and we can use that to spread love instead of anger. We can also learn to be more direct with our emotions, keep less bottled up, and choose better influences in our lives. Everyone can change, even *you*.

The first step to stopping the fighting is finding common ground. We are all girls, and we face many of the same challenges. If we can find better ways to share our troubles, communicate, and work together, there is no limit to what we can do.

"We have to look at each other as allies, not enemies, and rise above the media's messaging to us that says we have to hate other girls and women. What we need in this world right now is more unity and less cattiness. The only way we can change this is if we, each in our own way, begin to look at this issue and take action!"

° Jessica Weiner °

author and advice columnist

WORKING TOGETHER

When was the first time you saw girls join forces? Maybe when the girls in fifth-grade gym class played the boys in a fierce game of dodge ball? It didn't matter that 10 minutes before you lined up in the gym, Jennifer told you that you smelled, or that Rebecca glared at you from across class that morning after you screeched the chalk against the blackboard. You shoved your grudges and alliances aside, and worked as a team for one great cause — to pummel the boys!

You can do that now (work collectively, *not* pummel boys, that is). There are way too many important causes that could seriously use your help — like animal rights, school reform, environmental issues, domestic violence, and human rights. When girls form bonds instead of fissures, all of us not only stop fighting with each other, but also create positive change *together*.

"It takes some time to sort out the friends worth keeping, but once you do, they're life-savers."

Lisa Hix

magazine writer and Web producer

"It is important to know that, as females, we are a worldwide community still fighting for our right to be heard, to be respected, to be equal. Most girls and women feel a kinship with other girls, but some try and divide us. It is important to our advancement as a gender that we stick together as women and know that we are here for each other for support."

Jane Wiedlin

founding member, The Go-Go's

WHO, ME, A FEMINIST?

Do you believe that women deserve to be treated
as equals to men? Do you have love and respect for
yourself and your fellow "sisters"? Are you strong
and smart and ready to take on the world? If you
answered yes to any of these questions, you are,
indeed, a feminist. Most girls do not view themselves
as feminists, because they think that the term
implies that they are not feminine (even though the
two words are practically the same) or that they
can't have a boyfriend (so wrong — guys love strong
women). Feminists are just people who support
women and help to empower them. That pretty
much makes all of us girls feminists.

Why does it matter? Because feminism is based on
banding together. Feminists come in all shapes and
colors, from your best friend, who wants to be a
gynecologist because she cares about women's health;
to your grandma, who decades ago demanded the
same pay as the men she was working alongside; to
your little cousin who is planning to take over the
world with her Barbie; to your boyfriend's stay-
at-home mom who successfully raised four children
and loved every minute of it. Feminists can even be
guys who support the women in their lives (like your
boyfriend, though he may never admit it).

"I was lucky enough to find friends who were interested in feminism, and they taught me a lot about self-respect and caring for other girls and women. Every time I found myself thinking 'what a bitch,' I tried to remember that by using that word I was not respecting myself or other women of the world, and that this kind of thinking and speaking keeps women low on the food chain, so to speak.

"If women and girls don't look out for one another, no one else will! By constantly tearing one another down, we are participating in a system that is set up to keep women out of positions of power. And, power aside, hating on girls feels terrible for both the hater and the hated."

○ Emily Moeller ○

program director, Willie Mae Rock Camp for Girls

Feminism has a long history.

mid 1800s to early 1900s

First-wave feminism started in the mid-19th century and focused on securing higher education for women, gaining access to the professional workplace, winning property rights and child custody rights for unmarried women, and gaining the right to vote.

1960s to 1980s

Second-wave feminism spanned the 1960s through the '80s and mainly battled sex discrimination in the workplace. It included the 1963 landmark United States Equal Pay Act, which made it illegal to pay men and women different wage rates for equal work.

1990s to present

Third-wave feminism began in the '90s and has brought more attention to racial and ethnic minorities, as well as lesbians, and bisexual and transgender women. It has also challenged the earlier notion that feminists need to be career women, arguing that hard-working housewives and stay-at-home moms aren't any less valuable because they don't earn a paycheck.

In the Write

Writing has always been a primary outlet for activists *and* women, so it's no surprise that there have been so many feminist publications. In the early days, magazines like *Ms.*, *Sassy*, and *Lilith* led the way in feminist thinking. Later, edgier ones like *BUST*, *Bitch*, *Rockrgrl*, *American Girl*, *CRAFT*, and *Venus Zine* appeared on the scene.

Over the years, all sorts of subgenres of feminism have popped up. Some are:

○ **the Riot Grrrl movement**
girl power through self-expression and the indie/punk DIY movement

○ **eco-feminism**
nature-loving girls and women who support Mother Earth

○ **fashionista feminism**
girls who love clothes and beauty but also demand respect

○ **race feminism**
supports the uniting of all women of color

○ **ethnic/religious feminism**
supports the uniting of women of one particular ethnicity or religious faith

○ **radical feminism**
the idea that women are better off without men

○ **all-inclusive feminism**
feminism that gets men in on the party, too

HOW WE CAN START UNITING

Whether you embrace the word *feminism* or not, the point is to change your mindset so that you automatically develop feelings of mutual respect for every girl you meet. Everybody knows that girls rule … you just need to see every girl as a ruler in her own way. It takes some time to start retraining your mind this way, but it can change your life. You can start simply by being nicer to your younger sister or more empathic to your mom because you see them now as part of the gang and not enemies. Then, move outwards from there.

> "We're already a team, we just don't all realize it. There are so many areas of life in which it is still a man's world—sucks but it's true! Girls can be this incredible web of support for each other if we all just get into the mindset of holding out our hands to each other. How great would it be if all girls had each other's backs?"
>
> ° Isabel Samaras °
>
> painter

"Recognizing the
good in yourself when you're
a young woman can be very
difficult, especially when everything
around you tells you that you're not good
enough. I wish that I had been self-possessed
enough to know that the girls who were mean and
exclusive were often making up for their own
feelings of insecurity. I wish I could have known
that I rock, because knowing that about
yourself allows you to help other girls
and women feel like they rock.
And that's a great feeling."

○ **Emily Moeller** ○

program director, Willie Mae Rock Camp for Girls

There are a lot of ways to promote girl unity.
Here are some ideas:

- Embark on a girl-focused project, like ending the girl wars at your school.

- Play guitar in an all-girl band or start a zine about topics that you think girls would be into.

- Volunteer or intern at a female-run company or nonprofit organization.

- Become a member of a women's rights organization.

- Go to an all-girls arts or sports camp.

- Start your own pro-girl club at school.

See page 122 for more ideas.

"*I have been fortunate enough to be a member of The Devil-Ettes for nearly 10 years now. At first look, we're a bunch of kooky girls who love to dance, perform, wear fun costumes, and share a passion for glitter and vintage go-go boots. But if you ask any one of us what our fondest Devil-Ette memories are, the answer might surprise you. Of course we love thinking about all the cool places we've performed, but the best part has been the sisterhood we've developed.*"

Alexandra Tyler

writer and performer, The Devil-Ettes

DOES IT GET BETTER AFTER HIGH SCHOOL?

Yes … and no.

Yes, because you get to meet lots of new people after high school (perhaps in college or wherever you travel to), and just opening that field a little wider pretty much guarantees that you'll meet people who are more mature and nicer than the people you were forced to socialize with before.

Yes, also because you yourself are (hopefully) more mature and know better than to get involved in the girl wars and girl drama, even when other girls or women might egg you on.

But the answer is also no, not completely, because it's very hard to educate the entire world of women on how to play nice. As you move into the workplace, you may encounter some of the same behavior you dealt with in high school. Instead of fighting over boys, the women might be clawing for the only promotion, and instead of gossiping in the girls' bathroom, they might be doing it in the office kitchen or lounge.

"High school is only four years of your life. At the time, they seem like the most important years, but life gets so much more interesting and fun as you get older. It's always hard to imagine, but years later you look back and think, 'Wow, I can't believe I let those dumb girls get to me.'"

Alexandra Tyler

writer and performer, The Devil-Ettes

"As an adult, I try to hang around positive people, and if other people come up in conversation, I try to think of good things to say about them."

Elizabeth McGrath

lead singer for Miss Derringer and visual artist

Even though adults are supposed to be mature and, well, act like adults, many of them will send blind emails to other coworkers (without the sender's knowledge), shoot instant messages about neighboring coworkers from cubicle to cubicle, start rumors about someone's credibility in the workplace, or leave whiny notes on the office refrigerator (usually about stolen cookies or messy dishes left in the sink).

But it doesn't have to be this way forever. As the leaders of the next generation, you can effect change and make a huge difference in how women see each other just from changing how you act right now. Sure, all humans aren't perfect, but it's how we deal with our flaws that leaves the greatest impression on others. Leading by example may just help stop the cycle of female cruelty. Reading this book was the first step, and putting into action what you learned is the second.

With some effort and true understanding, you can make a difference not only for yourself, but also for the next generation of girls and women!

RESOURCES:
GET EMPOWERED!

Check out the websites and organizations listed below to see how you can get empowered and build strong relationships with other teen girls and women.

1. Girls Incorporated
www.girlsinc.org

Want to feel more empowered? This national non-profit youth organization can help. It's dedicated to inspiring all girls to be strong, smart, and bold, and helps girls use their own voices to promote positive change.

2. The Ophelia Project
www.opheliaproject.org

Susan Wellman's daughter committed suicide because of constant teasing and social torture, so she founded this project (named after the Shakespearean character Ophelia who committed suicide in *Hamlet*), which trains communities and schools in girl-on-girl cruelty. You can share stories here, too, about experiences you've had.

3. Girls For A Change
www.girlsforachange.com

Great organization for teen girls. Girls For A Change empowers thousands of girls to band together and create social change. Visit the site to see how you can make a difference.

4. World Association of Girl Guides and Girl Scouts
www.wagggsworld.org

Awesome girl-bonding opportunities here. This is a worldwide organization in which girls and young women develop leadership and life skills through self-development, challenge, and adventure.

5. About—Face
www.about-face.org

Lots of girl wars start because girls are competing over who looks better. About-Face teaches us that what we think is beauty is often based on harmful images we see in the media. The About-Face vision is to free girls and women from body-related oppression, so they will be capable of fulfilling their potential.

6. National Organization for Women (NOW)

www.now.org

Get political! NOW is the largest, most comprehensive feminist advocacy group in the United States. Has initiatives for young women in college.

7. National Women's History Project

www.nwhp.org

Go here to find out about all of the amazing things women have been doing together throughout history.

8. Feminist Majority Foundation (FMF)

www.feminist.org

Dedicated to equality, reproductive health, and non-violence, FMF empowers women economically, socially, and politically. FMF believes that feminists — boys and girls — are in the majority and just need the right support to get work done. Check out the student activism page.

9. Helping Our Teen Girls In Real Life Situations, Inc. (HOTGIRLS)

www.helpingourteengirls.org

Great resource for young black women. Has lots of girl-centered information and programming that's inspired by hip-hop and other aspects of teen culture.

ACKNOWLEDGEMENTS

When you write a book about how girls should stop hurting each other and start uniting, you quickly discover how many cool women there are who want to offer help.

First, I'd like to give a huge shout-out to the eclectic mix of women authors, artists, musicians, activists, athletes, and performers who contributed their advice and survival stories to this book. You are all my heroes and you rock!

Endless gratitude also goes to my best gal pal Kate for talking me through ideas and keeping me sane and to my favorite photographer Nicole Love for taking such a snazzy snapshot of me for this book.

Special thanks go to the awesome ladies of Orange Avenue Publishing — especially to publisher and creative director Hallie Warshaw and my editor, Karen Macklin, who helped keep me on track and focused.

Thanks to my mom, stepmom, and all the other women in my life who aren't afraid to be themselves. And last, thanks to a very special female incapable of ever giving the cold shoulder — my dog Sophie.

Photo by Nicole Love

Bonnie Burton

writes tips for teens on everything from
dating musicians to dealing with jealous best
friends on her site Grrl.com. She's written for
Bust, Geek Monthly, Star Wars Insider, and
Wired magazines, and contributed to the comic
anthology *The Girls' Guide to Guys' Stuff.*
Her previous books include *You Can Draw:
Star Wars* and *Never Threaten to Eat Your
Co-Workers: Best of Blogs.*
She lives in San Francisco.